T0053699

A IS FOR ACHOLI

Other titles by Otoniya J. Okot Bitek

100 Days

Gauntlet

A IS FOR ACHOLI

Otoniya J. Okot Bitek

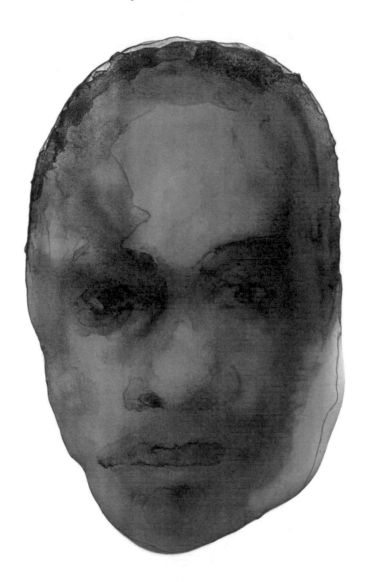

A Buckrider Book

© Otoniya J. Okot Bitek, 2022

No part of this publication may be reproduced, stored in a retrieval system or transmitted, in any form or by any means, without the prior written consent of the publisher or a license from the Canadian Copyright Licensing Agency (Access Copyright). For an Access Copyright license, visit www.accesscopyright.ca or call toll free to 1-800-893-5777.

Published by Buckrider Books
an imprint of Wolsak and Wynn Publishers
280 James Street North
Hamilton, ON L8R2L3
www.wolsakandwynn.ca

Editor for Buckrider Books: Paul Vermeersch
Editor: Canisia Lubrin
Copy editor: Peter Midgley
Cover image: *Julie* by Elizabeth MacKenzie
Layout: Kilby Smith-McGregor
Author photograph: Greg Black
Typeset in Freight Pro and Acumin Pro
Printed by Coach House Printing Company, Toronto, Canada

10 9 8 7 6 5 4 3 2 1

The publisher gratefully acknowledges the support of the Ontario Arts Council, the Canada Council for the Arts and the Government of Canada.

Library and Archives Canada Cataloguing in Publication

Title: A is for Acholi / Otoniya J. Okot Bitek.
Names: Okot Bitek, Otoniya J., author.
Description: Poems.
Identifiers: Canadiana 2022028542X | ISBN 9781989496558 (softcover)
Classification: LCC PS8629.K68 A75 2022 | DDC C811/.6—dc23

To S.T. and for us

Contents

An alphabet for the unsettled

I've been thinking diaspora is & is not
the us of home & how & where we're enough &
how this nation demands &
that nation extracts &
that other nation seeks but does not want us

to say hello ki leb Acholi
one might ask quite literally i tye
are you there
        do you exist
                are you

in response we might say   a tye
a tye ma ber
        I'm here I exist I'm good I'm fine I exist well

these poems are about that

An alphabet
for the unsettled

these days like loose threads like untied laces like
frayed edges like tenuous connection days like
remembrances days like bits we can only access
if we're to survive days that are untenable
palpable days pulsating through that prominent
vein on your temple days like memories you can't
hold onto like last tuesday which means nothing at
all except that there was a tuesday last week

An Acholi alphabet

A is for Acholi[1] Achol the Black one & the black one

A is for the apple that was lobbed at us from a garden far away & exploded in our compound

A is for me

---

[1] Adam
   My grandmother's oldest brother
   This means that I can trace my lineage back to this first man
   This means that the earth is young
   Or as I believed as a child my great-uncle was that old

B is for Acholi[2] that's who we are
B is for floor smeared in cow dung
B is for the floor with give

---

2   Beatitudes
    & other fables

C is for Acholi[3]

C is for stories like floors with give

C is for Acholi & British & Canadian ID papers

---

3   Cartography
    The trace of the arc of the apple to this point in time

D is for Acholi[4]
D is for the November fog & endless rain
D is for brown Vancouver Augusts

---

4   Devotion
    To family to self to nation & sometimes of another to us
    One day as we waited for the bus to Kampala a man very tall very dark white clothing red eyes
    There is your bus to Kampala he pointed
    We ran ran ran & after we had settled inside our mother asked if any of us had thanked him
    in our rush
    We looked back at the crowds
    How does such a presence of a man disappear

E is for Acholi[5]
E is for the human voice in the violin
E is for the catch of the Acholi dance

---

5   Externality
    A condition of always
    My mother tells us how her grandfather always told her everything I do I do for you
    My mother tells of when she was newly arrived in Canada how a man approached her and
    asked if she was the granddaughter of Mohamed Lagara
    You wear his face he told her something like that
    As a boy this man was the beneficiary of a kindness from my mother's grandfather
    All this time later the generosity of Mohamed Lagara would be part of a welcome to a
    country full of people who had no memory of who we were

F is for Acholi[6]
F is for small heaps of mango for sale by the roadside
F is for small tables of homemade brew also for sale by the roadside

`

---

6   Fixation
    On the thing that is always the thing in these parts
    The memo no employee can wear their hair in braids at work

G is for Acholi[7]
G is for dead poets & dead singers
G is for the music holding words we hang onto

     We only sing the songs we recall from childhood
     How we keep ourselves tethered with songs that our own children don't know

H is for Acholi[8]

H is for serendipity

H is for five-syllable words that mean nothing most days

---

8   Heresy
    Decades now we celebrate Thanksgiving
    Remember our delight when the Safeway turkey came with mash potatoes & cranberry sauce

I is for Acholi[9]

I is for the arc of that apple lobbed at us from the garden of Eden

I is for the arc of that apple

---

9   Inconstancy
    How else are we still here
    We bend to your traditions
    We hold Thanksgiving Dinner
    We forget that the Fort in Patiko held slaves
    But we remember that Samuel Baker's wife was named after the moon because of her white
    skin

J is for Acholi[10]
J is for hazy yellowy traffic lights through fog
J is for the reach of claws into your chest

---

10 Justice
    For who
    When
    Where

K is for Acholi[11]
K is for the April May mangoes
K is for also for elephant grass

---

11 Kitchen stories   my great-grandmother
    My mother's grandmother smoked pumpkins over the hearth for a couple of years at least
    according to my mother
    They might have looked terrible afterwards but you never tasted a sweeter pumpkin my
    mother tells me

L is for Acholi[12]
L is for the glory & rhythm of ostrich feathers
L is for the dance of the devil

M is for Acholi[13]

M is for naŋa the duet between the singer & the string

M is for the dead of an untouched drum

---

13   Maternal
      My great-grandmother lost her mother in a colonial war
      Which one
      We don't or can't remember
      There was fighting
      Gunshots
      The mother of my great-grandmother shot with the baby on her back
      My great-grandmother brought up by a stepmother that her father married afterwards
      You don't waste rice not a single grain she would tell her granddaughter my mother who told me
      We can't waste rice not even a single grain because the mother of my great-grandmother
      was shot with a baby on her back & did not grow up with that kind of affordance

N is for not Acholi[14] enough
N is for not British enough
N is for not Canadian enough

---

14 Nonsense

O is for Acholi[15]

O is for me who is always black

O is for Black & African

---

15 Open-ness

Last week a kid walking by adjusted the hoodie on his head & I felt his palm on my head

P is for Acholi[16]
P is for story beads
P is for the crater & the reverberation

---

16 Patience
    With the self
    With the unretracted claws
    See T is for Acholi
    T is for Temperance

Q is for Acholi[17]

Q is for the dances we missed all these decades

Q is for the songs that fell to the floor

---

17 Quest
    For the equality of silences within & without
    In the evening crows rise head west
    Sometimes they stop for a bit on the trees near 41st on Granville on the north side

R is for Acholi[18]
R is for the offence
R is for how little I care about your offence

18 Reconciliation
  With the buzz & the halo of the public word

S is for Acholi[19]

S is for the gates of unfreedoms

S is for gestures limited to the moneyed

    Whenever we heard sirens during the graveyard shift my co-worker would say
    Duck Julie
    They're coming for you

T is for Acholi[20]
T is for the mountains that race east
T is for the same mountains that hold us in

---

20 Temperance
    The goodness I must exhibit
    The goodness I must exhibit
    The goodness I must exhibit
    The goodness I must exhibit

U is for Acholi[21]

U is for cartography of stories

U is for the relationship between an apple & sin & a curse

---

21 Understatement
   To be invisible & hypervisible in this big black & Black body

V is for Acholi[22]
V is the for absolution
V is the for the first taste of apple

---

22 Veneration
    How our mother carefully unbound the apple from a piece of tissue she saved from work to
    share with us kids
    How powdery it was
    How it crumbled in our mouth
    How we wondered what the magic was
    The first sin was not knowing the apple

W is for Acholi[23]

W is for tethering of the maypole

W is for what keeps us bound to ourselves

---

23 Whereas
    Loaded & set to reveal what ways we will be kept away outside beyond & without

X is for Acholi[24]
X is for abstinence & refusal
X is for insistence

---

24 "eXterminate the brutes!"
    How Joseph Conrad writes us is impossible to forget

Y is for Acholi[25]

Y is for the unasked

Y is for everything we swallowed on the road from history to the present

---

25 Yellow
   For the same sun with its mockery of light
   What sort of witness is this

Z is for Acholi[26]

Z is for capacious

Z is for the gourds to hold that much meaning

---

26 Zeal

  To be seen

  In Gulu the graves of my great-grandparents Mohamed Lagara & Mamba & their daughters Juliate & Ajak lie in repose

  The middle of the grave is open to the sky my mother tells me in a tradition that believes we must not trap the souls of the people we love

A dictionary
for un/settling

so now I reckless I damned I candied I salt I tempered
I soft I terrified I terrified I terrified they said you
weren't dead yet I terrified that that might also be
true so I reckless now I given up I sullied I done they
said you're on the way back I terrified you bandied
you toughness you vented you fought you kicked you
beat you shouted you lied now I terrified that you're
here I terrified that you're here & I terrified that you're
here for good

so I reckless now painting my nails only after three
in the afternoon I doting on cats I watchful for new
news I watchful for the bizarre the whispered the
curse I dried hard I cracked I happened only in the
shatter oh gather oh lean in listen listen these are
only moments stacked up against atop beside each
other moments beaded like necklaces moments
incremental incidental instrumental sometimes dire
because dream because fate because old gods pointed
right not left oh gather & listen to this refuse this
stance this rejection this rant assemble now poets
now singers now crowd in the cords & the lyrics
in the back room where you stored tune & rhythm
assemble now poets singers & drummers where are
the dreams where's the tune & rhythm section

so reckless me thrown reckless me down reckless me
throned to moments without you in the periphery in
the distance or shadow at my door reckless me damned
reckless me sinner there was never anything else
offered in the clamour

If/once we were

any moor ^{any of us with our heads in our laps} drags his talons slowly ^{ever}
& seemingly deliciously ^{over}
    dry mounds _{in piles & piles} of skin

scraps of skin dead skins of any moor ^{any of us with our heads in our laps}
dead   white
& sometimes grey flakes
in a heap _{in piles & piles mounds even} on the _{carpeted} floor beneath his right leg

once ^{& only once}
once ^{& once again}
with
his c   a   v   e   r   n   o   u   s   voice over
                         e
        once ^{again again}   v
               e
           r
        y
      t
    h
  i   once ^{again again again}
 n
g
& e   v   e   r   y   o   n   e   o   n   c   e

           we were ^{are we are we are we are} people

Salt stories

Ash to salt
salt to land
land to sea
sea to sky
sky to story
story to land
land to threshold
threshold to step

& back & back & back
on this land & in time
what else but stave off the demons

Salt[1] to land[2] to sea[3] to sky[4] to story[5] to land[6] to threshold[7] to step[8]

---

1   Dionne Brand: *A Map to the Door of No Return: Notes on Belonging*

2   Leanne Betasamosake Simpson: *Dancing on Our Turtle's Back: Stories of Nishnaabeg Re-creation, Resurgence and a New Emergence*

3   Edwidge Danticat: *Krik? Krak!*

4   Claudia Rankine: *Citizen: An American Lyric*

5   Toni Morrison: *The Dancing Mind*

6   Saidiya Hartman: *Lose Your Mother: A Journey Along the Atlantic Slave Route*

7   M. NourbeSe Philip: *Zong!*

8   Cecily Nicholson: *From the Poplars*

Ash

having been locked to land & free to home   we discover ways to salt from ash
also salt licks also salt panning   what did we need the sea for
never bound by the ocean until the slavers came down the Nile   & marked us
us terrorized us enraged   us subdued   faces drawn yet still here still here   still

i can draw you a map

in 1862   emissaries of the sorcerer-queen arrived in Acholi   bearing gifts   as they do
show us your chief   your queen   your warriors   we asked of them   we
will not speak only with mercenaries   we told them we know the people stealers
         we know the elephant killers   who are you what are your intentions   what
do you trade in what are your laws   what are your stories   tell us these things or we will not
hold court with you

for four decades we were stolen of
people   & ivory & cattle stolen by
those from   Khartoum with their base
in Palaro &   Pabbo   & then by those
from the coast   from places like
                                                            Zanzibar

the emissaries showed us the image of the sorcerer-queen on glass they showed us the
king in the barrel they showed us the king on the cross & the king in the bounty
& went home to draw lines that mapped us differently

to make salt from ash is to live inside a story
to make salt from ash is to draw our own maps
this salt is our story
this ash is our means
i can point out the stars
& show you
how this is where we started

Salt

salt seeps out from land   into cement bags & rusted tins this is land to salt to
shanties toshantytowns   totears tosweat-stainedhandkerchiefs wiping
dusty foreheads in Nairobi streets

this is land to salt   to blood to red dust
land to map stories   land to salt stories

we never made it across the road
we were bound by mehndi patterns like maps of the places
we'd been to

round around round around   giddy & far too young to be looking for love
day's end children still laughing children still playing children chasing the train that races
through Kibera

    gari ya moshi
    inaenda mbele
    na mzigo yake
    tooo tooo

come city[1]   come county[2] come towns[3]   come boundaries[4]   come red roads[5]   come rust rails[6]

go train
go train
go
take our dreams with you
us we might never cross the street
us we may never arrive

---

1   Dar es Salaam haven of peace port of slave trade
     Dar es Salaam of the white sands of tourists love of Swahili of Tanzanite of love of everyday people of course

2   What did we ever know about countries except what they showed us in glass mirrors that they carried
     in their pockets

3   At Lamogi in 1911 the last of Acholi resistance against British colonialism ended with the suffocation of
     54 men, 28 women & 30 children at the Guruguru caves where they'd barricaded themselves
     In 1915 my great-grandfather an employee of the colonialists arrived in Gulu to work as an administrator
     Gulu was founded as a town that year
     The hot springs there gurgled guru guru guru guru
     They were drained in the name of development

4   At Berlin in 1884 wasn't there a single African leader sitting with Europeans to map out a continent

5   During the dry season red dust rises off the road creating a fantastic silhouette of the world
     We cover our faces with kerchiefs headscarves & kitenge as we ride at the back of trucks hitching a ride
     from Wii Gweng to Kitgum
     We drop the cloth as we step off onto the road thanking the driver
     All our eyes are masked with red powder our days with broken & rusted testimony & our nights with
     lust for beauty

6   Our great-uncle returned from the war in Kenya bearing colourful plastic basins from Nakuru
     He came by train he said
     There was no memory of trains until we dug out the tracks

in Mombasa   tales arrive in sacks on the backs of men that off-load sacks unload tears
off-load sacks unload story off-load sacks   unload craters   unload boxes   unload bales
unload paper off-load sacks   unload the tallest of lies in crystal form   all bubble wrapped
& precious   on the way to prestigious museums abroad
upload
upload
upload
horns   fantasy   white sand

land to sea bones
land to sea salt
land to sea cries
of excitement &
shanties

this is a map to the salt lines beyond borders that lead to my home

Sky[1]

the thing that was there is the thing itself which is this
there was a story itself the thing
two shadows walk with me   hand in hand   our feet in step
these shadows are the thing itself
there's warmth between us who are the thing that is this story
we know that the orbit of stars does not depend on this love or any other
we hurtle to nothing

---

1   This is the road from Vancouver to Whistler in British Columbia Canada
    This is the road that men built
    This is the road that men built
    This is the road that men built
    This is the road we cut out of forests that had had the view of the sky for millennia
    This is the road we blasted into being
    This is the road whose walls are held up with chain links so that angry rocks don't fall into traffic
    This is the road that men built
    This is the road that required men to pay to come across the sea by head by tax by head tax
    This is the road that was expanded for the 2010 Olympics also in Whistler also in Vancouver
    This is the umbilical cord between city & town
    This is the road that men built died on & were buried in
    This is the Sea to Sky highway from coast to heaven
    This is the road that men built

Story

we landed with nothing into nothing & onto nothing we came to nothing spaces with
nothing people speaking nothing words doing nothing things looking at us with nothing in
their eyes

us with stories unpacked in envelopes photo albums us with skin that had yet to tingle when
the sun was right where was it we found ourselves again
what was this place whose stories we could not yet hear

we spoke into our own mouths[1] taking eating doing this in memory of us[2] in church we
swallowed our words like the body & blood[3] looked up at pink-hued sunsets moons with rust
rings that reminded us of salt

these days we ghost lines we ghost the lines on wednesdays we line up we line up
we line up we snake around the block waiting for a turn & then we turn & then we
turn & then we turn & turn & turn & we're gone

---

1   We spoke ourselves into being
    How else would we know that we were alive

2   Like Christ like Christ

3   Like Christ like Christ

To land

snakeplantsare air-cleaning plants bounds in pots & sold at the grocery store the gardening centre the hardware store these plants will clean the air in your house & in your bedroom

butsnakeplantsarealsosold
in potsalongtheroadtokabalagalainkampala
these plants will clean the air polluted by traffic these plants will clean the air polluted by stale stories these plants will clean the air polluted by lies these plants will clean the air polluted by nightmares of never-ending documents that require signatures snake plants will clean the air bound in pots made elsewhere snake plants will set you free

Threshold

whereskinsmeet wherestoriesclashor
sometimescometogetherinthe gentlest
&
sweetest
ways
tellmeastory[1]

---

1   In your beginning was the Word your word your name your language
    In the beginning was the Word & the word was Arrogance

& back & back & back

so now we've resorted to drawing daisies
a circle
a loop back
a loop back
touching the centre
then moving away & back home
loop at the elbows loop at the elbows
we're dancing we're dancing again

Step

in the long winter that we will not write about our stories were thrown across living rooms
pages flailing books landing on brute floors or ghost floors or the floor with a spatter of
green paint in the corner from the last time the wall was painted
those at home told us that they were tired of us & our stories
step over that ditch & you're gone

Excavating[1] Joseph Conrad's
Heart of Darkness

Three letters at a time

"Dark h   n sh   s c   d be made out in the dis   ce, fl   ing in   tinctly
a   nst the gl   y b   er of the fo   t, and near the r   r two br   e fi   es,
le   ng on tall s   ars, s   d in the su   ght u   r fan   tic he   - resses of
sp   ed s   s, w   ike and s   l in stat   que re   e. And from r   t to left
a   g the li   ed s   e m   d a wild and gor   us ap   ition of a w   n.
"She w   ed with me   red s   s, dr   d in st   ed and fri   d cl   s, tre   ng
the e   h pr   ly, with a sl   t ji   e and fl   h of bar   ous orn   nts. She
ca   ed her head high; her hair was done in the s   e of a he   t; she had b   s
leg   gs to the knee, b   s wire gau   ets to the e   w, a cri   n spot on her
t   y c   k, innu   able ne   aces of g   s b   s on her neck; bi   re t   gs,
c   ms, g   s of wi   -men, that hung about her, gli   red and tr   led at e   y
step. She must have had the v   e of se   al ele   nt t   s upon her. She was
sa   e and su   b, w   -eyed and mag   cent; t   e was som   ing om   us
and st   ly in her del   rate pro   ss. And in the hush that had fa   n su   enly
upon the w   e sor   ful land, the im   se wil   ness, the co   sal body of
the fe   d and m   erious life se   d to look at her, pe   ve, as th   h it had
been lo   ng at the i   e of its own te   rous and pass   ate soul.
"She came ab   st of the st   er, s   d s   l, and f   d us. Her long sh   w fell
to the wa   's edge. Her face had a tr   c and fi   e as   t of wild so   w and
of dumb pain mi   ed with the fear of some str   ling, half-sh   d res   e.
She s   d lo   ng at us wit   t a stir, and like the wil   ness it   f, with an
air of b   ding over an ins   table pu   se. A w   e mi   e p   ed, and then
she made a step for   d. T   e was a low ji   e, a g   t of ye   w m   l, a sway
of fri   d dr   ries, and she st   ed as if her h   t had fa   d her. The y   g
fe   w by my side gr   ed. The pil   ms mu   red at my back. She lo   d at

---

1   With gratitude to M. NourbeSe Philip for the teaching about the profane in the text & the
    work required for cleansing. To Jordan Abel for illustrating the poison through excavating
    the archive.

us all as if her life had de   ded upon the uns   ving ste   ness of her g   ce.
Su   nly she o   ed her b   d arms and t   w them up r   d above her head,
as th   h in an unc   rollable d   re to t   h the sky, and at the same time the
swift sh   ws da   d out on the e   h, s   t ar   d on the r   r, gat   ing
the ste   r into a sh   wy em   ce. A for   able si   ce hung over the s   e.
"She tu   d away sl   y, w   ed on, fol   ing the bank, and p   ed into the
bu   s to the left. Once only her eyes gle   d back at us in the dusk of the
thi   ts be   e she disa   ared.'

Of course, she did

She

she walked on

She x 33

she wild & she gorgeous
she of a she woman apparition
she measured she steps
she treading the she earth proudly
she carried she head she high
she value of several she elephant she tusks
she savage & she superb
she wild-eyed & she magnificent
she ominous & she stately
she tragic & she fierce
she like the she wilderness she self
she eyes gleamed she back at she in the she dusk
she talked like she a she fury

And

"   ,   ,and   ,
                    ,   ,   and
        . And   and   .
"   ,   and   ,   ,
and   .   ;   ;
                ,   ,   ,
        ;   ,   ,   ,   ,   and
    .   .   and   ,   and
    ;   and   . And
                    ,   ,   and
            ,   ,   and   .
"   ,   ,and   .   '   .   and
            and   .
        ,and   ,   .   ,and
                    .   ,   ,   ,and
    .   .   .
                    .   and   ,
                    ,and
        ,   . A formidable silence hung over the scene.
"   ,   ,   and
        .   .
"   ,   ,   '
                    .   and
                ,   .   ,   ,
        and   .   .   ....   _ ,   .   ,
    , ,   , .

Ah, well

"   ,   ,
                    ,   ,   ,
              .
"   ,   ,   ,
              .   ;   ;   ,
              ,   ,   ;   ,   ,
              ,   ,   .
         .   ,   ;   .
                                   ,   ,
                         ,   ,
"   ,   ,   .   ,   .
                                                                            .
         ,   ,   .   ,
              .   ,   ,   ,
              .   .   .
                                                       .
         ,   ,
         ,   ,   .   .
"   ,   ,
         .
"   ,   ,   '
                                   ;   ,   .
                                   .
                         .   .   ,
              ,   .   .   ,
                    , ...   – '   . Ah, well,
it's all over now.'

How she talked

         ,   ,

  ,   ,   ,

         .   .

"   ,   ,   ,

      .   ;   ;   ,

    ,   ,   ;   ,   ,

    ,   ,   .

  .   ,   ;   .

        ,   ,   .

"   ,   ,   .   .

   ,   ,   .   ,

     .   ,   ,   ,

    .   .

      .

  ,   ,

  ,   ,   .   .

"   ,   ,

  .   .

"   ,   , '

          .

   .   .   , she talked like a fury   ,

       .   ,

   , ... – '   . ,

, ,   ,   .

A whole minute

in the hush that had fallen suddenly
a whole minute passed

she stood still
a whole minute passed

& faced us
a whole minute passed

she stood looking at us
a whole minute passed

the pilgrims murmured
the pilgrims murmured
the pilgrims murmured
a whole minute passed

a formidable silence hung over the scene
a whole minute passed
a whole minute passed
a whole minute passed
a whole minute passed

& then she made a step forward

**Dark human shapes could be made out in the distance,
flitting indistinctly**

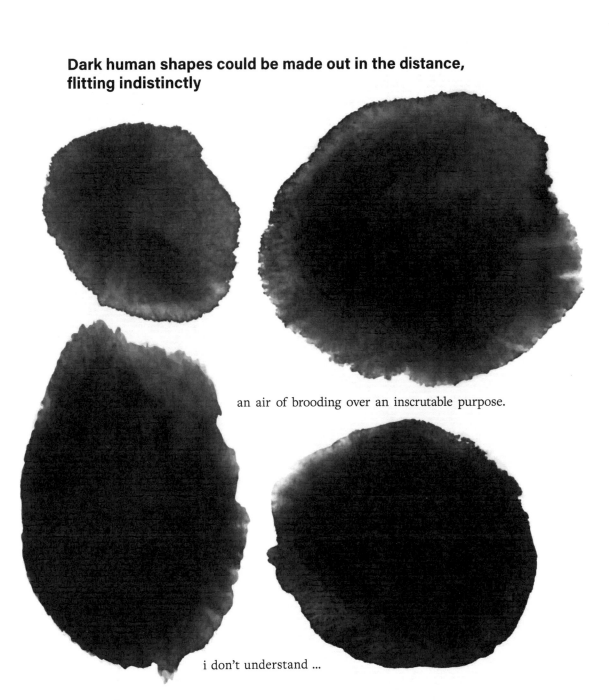

an air of brooding over an inscrutable purpose.

i don't understand ...

Dark human shapes

D could be made out in the distance
A could be made out in the distance
R could be made out in the distance
K could be made out in the distance

H flitting indistinctly
U flitting indistinctly
M flitting indistinctly
A flitting indistinctly
N flitting indistinctly

S warlike
H warlike
A warlike
P warlike
E warlike
S warlike

dark human shapes could be made out in the distance flitting indistinctly
warlike warlike warlike warlike
warlike warlike warlike warlike
like dark human shapes warlike
like war like war like war like
human like dark dark dark war like
war like

dark human shapes like war shapes
like war shapes like war shapes
like war like human like dark
human like war
human war
human war
human
like   like
like   like

Apparition of a woman

Apparition of a woman   Apparition of a woman   Apparition of a woman

Apparition of a woman   Apparition of a woman   Apparition of a woman

Apparition of a woman   Apparition of a woman   Apparition of a woman

Apparition of a woman   Apparition of a woman   Apparition of a woman

Apparition of a woman   Apparition of a woman   Apparition of a woman

Apparition of a woman   Apparition of a woman   Apparition of a woman

I really think I would have tried to shoot her

Apparition of a woman   Apparition of a woman   Apparition of a woman

I don't understand

Apparition of a woman   Apparition of a woman   Apparition of a woman

Ah well, it's all over now

"she walked jingle and flash of barbarous had failed. the young fellow by resolve. she stood looking my side growled. the pilgrims my back. ss beads on her neck; bizarre fortnight to keep her out of things, charms, gifts of witch-m"dark human shapes in the distance, flitting indistinctly" ead-dresses of spotted skins, warlike and still in statuesque r her epose. and from right to left along the lighted shore moved a wild and gorgeous apparition of a woman. en, that hung nd stately in her de and, and like the wilderness itself, with an air of brooding over anhboard i really think i would have tried to shelbow, a crimson spot on her tawny gathering the steamer into a cheek, if her heart slight innumerable necklaces of gla draperies, and she stopped as hhe river two bronze figures, murmured at leaning on tall spears, stood in the sunlight under fantastic een that, for she talked like a fury to kurtz for an hour, pointing at me now come a against the gloomy band understander,' said thelibed khigh; her hair was done in the shapnd mysteriouabout her, glittered and trembled at every step. she must have had the value of se treading veral elephant tusks upon her. she was, wild-eye d and magnificent; thing ominous as lifet least it must have b inscrutable witch-m"dark human purpose. a w sorrowful land, the immense wilderness, the colossal body of the fecund hole minute passed, and then she made. or there would have beethere was a low jingle, a glint of her luckily for me eyes gleamed back at us in the dusk of the thickets before she disappeared.oot with in striped and fringed a step forward cloths, the earth proudly, with a e of a helmet; to the knee, her tawny cheek brass wire gauntlets to the ving stead her bared arms wholeaornaments. she carried her head as could be made out though in an uncontrollable desire to touch the sky, savage superb and at the time the swift shadows darted out on the e ""if she had offered to come a against the gloomy border of the forest, and near t tz felt too ill that day to care, yellow metal, a swft. once only n mischief. i don't understand . . gress. and in passed into the the hush that had fallen suddenly measured steps, draped upon the ad been looking at the image of its own tenebrous and passionate soul.then.i don't "she came abreast of ling, half-shaped at us without a stir man of patches, nervously. 'i have been risking my life every day race. a fo . . no – seemed to look at her, pensive, she had brass leggings as though it her long shadow fell to hand threw them up rigid above iness of her glance. suddenly she opened her head,icked up a row about those miserable rags i pickerate prorm same idable silence hung over the scene."she turned away slowly, walked on, following the bank, and bushes to the leeroom to mend my clothes with. i wasn't decent. ait's too much for mefor the last the house. sh was somr face had ae and of dumb pain mingled with the fear of some struggs all as if her life had depended upon the unswerarth, swept around on the river, gathering the steamer into a shadowy emb. he dialect of this tribe., i fancy kurte got in one day and up in the storay of fringedshe looked at uthe steamer, stood still, and faced us. the water's edge. he tragic and fierce aspect of wild sorrowthere Ah, well,

it's all over now.'

Flitting indistinctly

Dark human shapes^{flitting indistinctly}
two bronze figures^{flitting indistinctly}
striped and fringed clothes^{flitting indistinctly}
measured steps^{flitting indistinctly}
brass leggings^{flitting indistinctly}
a crimson spot^{flitting indistinctly}
wild sorrow^{flitting indistinctly}
dumb pain^{flitting indisctinctly}
half-shaped resolve^{flitting indisctinctly}
mysterious life^{flitting indisctinctly}
a glint of yellow metal^{flitting indisctinctly}
uncontrollable desire^{flitting indisctinctly}
a formidable silence^{flitting indistinctly}
dusk of thickets^{flitting indistinctly}
the man of patches^{flitting indistinctly}

I don't understand

Settled/unsettled

Resettle

resettle
to settle again
to start again
to begin all over again
in direction in wind

in sheets on a clothesline
your life
whipped about
flapped about
whipped about
flapped about

tell me
is there is no woodsmoke in these parts

Resettlement

resettling officer
one who helps you fill out forms
one who helps you re-settle
one who knows social services
one who knows court appearances

fold up the sheets from the clothesline
hold them up to your fate
hold them up to your face
hold them up to the sky
hold them up to the tree
hold them up to the sound of playing children
hold them up to the bills
hold them up to the calendar
hold them up to the stove
hold them up to the dusty windowsill

he's not coming the resettlement officer says

settle in

Re-turned

resettled
to be turned
to be re-turned
to be unturned

guess what's a word   the child asks
what   you respond
insouciance
what does it mean   you ask
i don't know the child says
it just feels good in my mouth

like sweets in my mouth   the child says
rolling the word
in her mouth

Unsettled

unsettled
as in disturbed
stopped or still
in process
the mountains out in the rockies are unsettled

why you say that the child asks

because they haven't stopped moving
the mountains are in a race to the east coast

what's in the east coast   the child asks

your father
your father is in the east coast
your father is like the mountains
your father is like the rockies
your father also
hangs onto the sea
that's how come there are sea fossils in the rockies
that's how come they're so far away from the coast
that's how come your father carries a round pebble in his pocket
that's how come the wind blows as it does
that's how come the breeze is a kiss
the wind a sneeze to remind us
that the smell of woodsmoke is also a haunting

Settled

you settled you say
you're rich now

are you you extended
are you you big
are you you fluid
are you you got
are you you measure
are you you slim
are you you better
are you you better
are you you better

when flight took
did you soar

Anti-settler

anti-settler
    of course
the best days are bygone
the fifties were the best decade

There's something about

... Vancouver

there's something about vancouver something about freedom something
about dignity about being a woman today & about how a good education will
save you something about god prayer faith about the strong traditions of
your people about african culture & black girl magic about black pride like
you know be proud of yourself

something about the importance of economy about working hard about
capital something about shadow about colonialism about our aboriginals
about our first nations people
about
ours
ours
ours
ours
ours
ours

there's something
about that meme floating about online that spreads the romance of african
people who learn each other's songs & use them to fend off evil that has
been beautifully packaged as ubuntu &

of course of course the entire world singing bob marley's one love one heart
let's get together & feel alright

there's something about the language of belonging about memory justice
healing about opportunities to begin again in a new country

there's something about welcoming refugees
about the quebec minister of something something
telling us that women should not wear the hijab
because wearing the hijab means women are not free to wear what they want
so women must not be told what to wear
because they are free to wear what they want
but not the hijab because she says so

there's something about how face coverings are now required
something about those face coverings or masks
or whatever language is in vogue
is a declaration of care of you for me of me for you

something about being in this together in this country that's as white as dana
claxton's buffalo bone china & as old as old stock canadians

& for sure for sure for real there's something about buddy
something about buddy riding a bike towards me those two weeks ago on
main & first
something about the way buddy gets off his bike & addresses me directly
about not belonging here
& i'm all what
because i think i mishear
& buddy is you don't belong here you're a n*****
& w/out hesitation i know that this is an asshole move
& i call it for what it is
& i'm you're an asshole

& buddy's you're n*****
& i'm you're an asshole
& buddy is two steps away
& i can smell all of last week on buddy
but i stand I goddamn stand
as buddy holds on to a bike that's mute
& we're a vortex around which vancouver spins
& traffic whirrs on & pedestrians walk on by
as buddy & i scream at each other
& i turn as buddy walks away
with the bike a reluctant witness
& buddy hurls the word at me
this time with no pronoun
just vile just bile
n*****!
n*****!
n*****!
& i'm screaming back
asshole asshole asshole
& i have the last word
& i turn to keep on my way

& two women's eyes meet mine
& look away

so there's something about chill
something about it's not so bad

something about could've been way worse
something about maybe drunk maybe mental illness maybe stress
maybe   you know   the usual

something about citizenship
about freedom to be whoever you want to be today
about dignity & taking the high road
about privilege & family & good friends & continuous & never-ending hail
marys
& something about my girlfriend who tells me
swear to god I can walk with you to the police station right now & report this
& there's something about
i can't believe this kind of shit happens in vancouver today omg are you alright

& the sea to sky highway
& the so-called superiority of western culture & economy & capital
& opportunity & hard work & forgiveness & generosity
& something about if it's so so bad why don't you go back to whatever the hell
hole you came from

& mostly gratitude gratitude for the ancestral makeup of skin
of this skin that still holds me in
& this skin that keeps me together this skin that keeps me whole

... Today

there's something about today that is at once every day & also just today
something about today that gels or scatters or crystalizes or muds over
something about splendour about light
about shaking off   shirking off beating off   sweeping away
something about incredulity
something about loss
something about dates about moments   years
something about a century in the making many many centuries in the making
something about unity
something incredible about the idea that we're one & the same one & the same one &
the same one & the same
that it happened to you & to me
that we all suffered that we all suffered
that my heartbreak & yours come from the same place
there's something about the singular truth that will not be disputed by vast
tributaries each from a rivulet a stream a pond a hole in the ground where we buried
our dreams
where some seeded & grew into shrubs with pink flowers red a deep purple &
glorious yellow

sing me a song
sing me a song about your sister
sing me a song about your sister who won't speak now but dances
about the one who won't dance but digs the garden in rhythm with her own breath
about the one who won't hold a hoe but guides children
look at the board
look at the page

follow the line with your finger
about the one who won't teach but will judge with a strong gavel
guilty   not guilty   guilty   not guilty
about the one that will not judge but prays for us sinners all the time
about the one who won't pray but insists on fact and decries prejudice
about the one with her hair dyed red who walks among traffic whispering &
pointing & sometimes laughing at comedy that only she can hear
sing me a song about the claim that we won't we can't ever forget
but what is it that we want to remember

there's something about hauntings that persist
there's something about latency in the shoulder of a person who used to care
there's something about a thread
something about weaving
about reckoning
about sewing
about giving & pulling giving & pulling back
there's something about the need to hold on
something in that detail
a missing third fingernail on his left-hand fingertip now gnarled
sometimes he chews at it
sometimes he forgets about it
sometimes it takes him back to the moment when the car door slammed on his finger
how he couldn't pull his finger out
how he screamed
how the adults shouted
how someone banged at the car

how the car stopped having not really gone yet
how he howled
how he pained
how he never thought he'd ever forget
oh my god   oh my god

what are these things that you ask us to remember when we hold these
stories in our bodies
the confidence of statues
the weight of monuments
the red of the forever flame
the speeches
the trees that were planted
in line after line after line after line over two decades ago
look at the trunks of these trees
look at how youthful they are
look at how strong they are
look at how similar their heights are
same species aren't they
look at how by standing in the same spot each tree spans towards a horizon
look at heaven within their reach
look at all the possibilities
all the possibilities all of them

look
look
look

can you even imagine

... Thick sludge

there's something about the thick sludge of time today

something undulating

something uncompromising

something tight

something about lethargy

about sadness like a constant keen about heartbreak about debt about illness about sorrow

& there will always be something unforgiving about knees as weapons eight minutes long

about mothers

about ancestors

something about kneeling afterwards as political supplication

all striped all masked all ideology all heads bowed

with kente kente kente cloth draped about shoulders

we love Black people today

we love Black people today

we love Black people today

there's something about kneeling that's not to be confused with kneeling as fervour

like the mother of god

like the girlfriend of the mother of god

like the girlfriend of god at the base of the cross

in tears in prayer in defiance

of the armed ones who man the stage

because there's a chance that crossed men could step off

& go about their lives

there's something about mothers & ancestors & prayer

& the tennis players who tells it

I will not play

I will not play

I will not play

I will not play

play play play tennis play

games play

nice play

time play

power play

bets play

escape play

white skirts & upper arm strength

I will not play ball

there's something about the spin the curve the speed of the ball skimming the net

something about nets
about fish about
oceans about ships about
continental seaboards
& statues at the harbour
at the square at city hall

there's something about today that is likely to be forgotten
something about memory like a pall
or fishnet stockings torn at the knee of the girl with a bruised face
who will not talk about it though no one will ask
there's something about the yours-ness in the body of another
something about a knee
an afro a
power fist a
rejection a
claim a
fatal moment

there's something about rejection about
the refusal to name something about
call in the roll that that claims us all in this moment
that we will all but forget

The lock poems

Lock 1

a ghost sits at the base of my neck
aches
as present as presence as now

the butterfly is gone

Lock 2

market of dreams of markets in dreams for markets for dreams out of market out of dreams inside markets inside dreams because markets because dreams into markets also dreams

the baskets at the grocery store for sale have tags with the names & faces of the weavers from across the world
also prices in dollars

the beef at the butchers is from a cow named Rosie who was much loved & hand fed organic grass
also prices in dollars

Lock 3

ghost fathers with mournful faces do nothing for the state of the world

& all you men with adult progeny
& all you men still alive
& all of you holding your faces
& this is the state of the world

Lock 4

the losing season is here again
there goes my yellow pen green tunic favourite silk scarf newest poem that fell into
a cavern sixty days beyond daytime

here comes my recurring nightmares
the losing season is a familiar dread
so here we go again

Lock 5

I am dog
pronouncing death to the procrastinator

only on tuesdays
can I be woman
barking barking barking
the flowers are long gone
as are the children
there are no songs left of black

Lock 6

now that I have become the poet with the clapped head
hoofed feet
clawed claws
& dammed throat

now that my eyes are screwed shut
ears padlocked off
& navel sewn tight

I can only &
will only
write about flowers
& daylight
from memory

I refuse to be witness

Lock 7

after battle after battle after battle they return to the same spot same question
what is beauty

women with ravaged bodies eyes blackened
unsmiling & gaunt beyond slender

this is what women look like after war
this is what women should look like after war

this is women
after they were told
that beauty was their gaunt selves
this is women after after after after they were told
that there was no magic in the flesh of their self

Lock 8

a thumb lock at my nape
now a powerful force around me
there's nothing nothing nothing for you unless I allow it
unless I want it unless I decide that you can come in

break off my thumbs now still locked
break off all our thumbs & I'm still locked
I will myself into being & I will myself out
this is nothing nothing here
that you can ever touch again

Lock 9

sister grabs mother by the scruff of her neck
sister is mother's mother
sister drops mother at her feet demands of her look at me now mother looks at
sister & I interject stop stop now leave mother alone
sister unhearing grabs mother by the shoulder now speak now mother speak

mother stutters
speak stop speak stop speak stop speak stop
mother stutters mother's mother shouts stop speak stop speak
I on top of my lungs
I on my knees
stop speak stop stop stop stop stop
mother & sister both inside my throat
my nails at my own bloody neck

Lock 10

a chain
a muscle a chain
a bind a muscle
a grave a bind
fishbowl a grave
wedding ring a fishbowl

a chain
a muscle
a bind a chain
a grave a muscle
a marriage a grave
wedding bells a marriage

a chain
a muscle
a bind a chain
a grave a muscle
vows a grave
marriage bed wedding bells

Jacob's breath

at night the
floor rises to wrestle us
we fight like jacob & his demon his angel his god
we awake newly named
& limp towards morning night falls again
everywhere rising from shadows to dials to faces
& chokes about our necks
& we can't breathe for all this light

marking time marking place marking dates & space & how we feel weight at this time
write they say write it all down
write what you can mark the day
note time & it's already night

these days will take score give us reason to remember
or forget the excoriation
the disbelief the gravity the headlines the lock the door the clock & the floor
rises
to
wrestle
us

we
fight
like
jacob

& his demon
& his angel
& his god

we write as markers as those who decide when we awake or when we remain asleep
we write as gods naming recognizing hailing the newly named raising misremembering
we write as scribes with faith & fate & fervour & limp across with pen as crutch as marker
we write towards morning having wrestled all night like jacob & his demon his angel god
we write & night falls & day rises & night falls again
diurnal nocturnal dead & alive both dead as alive
switched on turned off rested
exhausted doors lock words dock clock clock
clock everywhere
until we understand that these days these nights don't end we do

what is ours but our own breath given taken given taken
what is ours but our own breath
foggy & rising
what is ours but our own breath soft or harsh
silent but for the whoosh that comes from inside ourselves
& then release & then permeation & then life like days & nights
like shadows silhouettes
translucence shimmer tricks of light like
dials like time like friendship like all markers we've adopted to write our lives into being

here's to faces to graces to places we've been spaces we've marked with our breath
here's to the choke the gasp the pen falling away how do we mark these times these
days this moment how do we go about our lives given the temerity the audacity the
anti-gravity of mediocrity the demands for our necks on the line in the way off the
course as others fail up as others kneel & we are the ones again marking marching
marking marching we can't we can't we can't we can't we're already marking our
present into the future breathe life mark life & we can't breathe & when we can't
live we mark & we march we mark mark mark mark mark on the single page writing
ourselves into being breath on the page for those who can't yet breathe & for those who
won't & for those who insist that we take it all
because it's ours anyway & the window remains locked from the outside & groans &
laughter is how we understand this place this notch this case
this this this our one
& i'm already my own god self
not waiting for light or time not wrestling not arguing not demanding
i'm already jacob already song already named already my own future self

Postscriptum

just like that six twenty three am & english is gone snatched from our tongues along with every single word that was rickrolled into our expressions which was never cool & now it's all gone gone gone from the radio from tv from the internet from book[1] spines & between covers surely i think to myself not the religious texts i needed to have in the house like the koran[2] like the bible[3] but look all done with english all emptied out all nothing except for the title[4] & names of god & angels[5] places & prophets[6] they too are bereft of the word of god[7] because they were written in english & now the only books[8] that remain are the ones in our tongue also atlases[9] & folded street maps with very very few names that we'd come to think of as natural to place & of course picture books[10] & now in these days of this thing perhaps we might begin to think of

---

1   the only books that remain are those in our tongue
     a reflection of the languages that are left in this house

2   the only books that remain are those in our tongue
     a reflection of which gods who live in this house

3   the only books that remain are those in our tongue
     a reflection of what saviours to forget in this house

4   the only books that remain are those in our tongue
     a reflection of what ghosts survive in this house

5   the only books that remain are those in our tongue
     a reflection of something soft in this house

6   the only books that remain are those in our tongue
     a reflection of the life to find in this house

7   the only books that remain are those in our tongue
     a reflection of the poets who live in this house

8   the only books that remain are those in our tongue
     a reflection of who we remember in this house

9   the only books that remain are those in our tongue
     a reflection of Abila & Anu in this house

10   the only books that remain are those in our tongue
     a reflection of symbols that echo & echo & echo in this house

ways to talk with each other across[11] & from inside our bodies & from our hearts & from our fingers pointing at stuff & us agreeing between ourselves on what we will call it if we must & how we will rename the world & more & in these days of this thing we might remember that we're still here we're still here we're still here & our tongues will carry the rhythm of how we came through[12] all those past apocalypses & how we will learn to draw maps again & how history can & will be challenged with more of our own stories in our own languages because because because we now know a world without empire

---

11   with gratitude to Ngũgĩ wa Thiong'o

12   & more gratitude & joy to M. NourbeSe Philip

Acknowledgements

It isn't possible to live in the Black diaspora without the love and support of family, friends and community who remind me that Acholi is an expansive way of being in the world. All these people, more, have held me in sustained friendship and family relation and I'm grateful to them. *A Is for Acholi* is for all of us who struggle with place, time and identity.

Thank you, Canisia Lubrin, for clearing the thicket to show me what *A Is for Acholi* was wanting to be, and for modelling friendship, work and brilliance through an unwieldy manuscript. Peter Midgley, thank you for saying yes, again, for polishing these poems to a shine and for many conversations about the work of words. Elizabeth MacKenzie, through your *Julie* series, I'm reminded how abstraction, too, is language and form. Thank you for the beautiful cover image. Thank you, Noelle Allen and Paul Vermeersch, for generosity and patience, and for making space for this book. I'm so appreciative of the support from the folks at Wolsak and Wynn.

The first glimpse I had of this book was at The Baldwin House Residency in Burnaby, BC, as part of the Shadbolt Fellowship and Simon Fraser University Writer-in-Residence Program. I'm grateful for the time, space and beauty I was accorded in the fall of 2020 and spring of 2021 to parse out this work.

This a small web of friendship and gratitude for support in getting me here: Ayumi Goto, Ashok Mathur, Peter Morin, Fatima Jaffer, Sarah Shamash, Veda Prashad, Kaie Kellough, always Barbara Binns, Sophia Malczewska, Sophie McCall, David Chariandy, Erin Baines, Pilar Riaño-Alcalá, Cecily Nicholson, Josema Zamorano, Peter Midgley, Sam McKegney, Diriye Osman, Katherine McKittrick, Lara Rosenoff Gauvin, Stephen Collis, Elizabeth MacKenzie, Elizabeth Schaeffer, Clint Burnham, Canisia Lubrin, Christina Sharpe, M. Neelika Jayawardane, Chantal Gibson, Denita Arthurs, Anakana Schofield, Beth W. Stewart, Koju Kasera, Kalina Lawino, Phanuel Antwi, James Gifford, Susan Lord, Seasmain Taylor, M. NourbeSe Philip, Jordan Abel, Ketty Anyeko, Lyse Lemieux, Jónína Kirton, Cissie Fu, Erin Soros. Pádhraic Ó Raghallaigh, for hearth and home.

All my siblings know these stories and they work very hard to keep me honest. In particular, and by proximity: Olga Bitek Ojelel, Cecilia Okot Bitek Johnson and David Lamony.

Many of these poems are inspired by stories from my maternal side of the family, through our mother, Caroline Okot Bitek, the ultimate storyteller and history keeper. Thanks, Mum.

Notes

Poems 1–5 in "Settled/unsettled" were previously published in *Cascadia Magazine*, November 12, 2019, www.cascadiamagazine.org/author/juliane-okot-bitek/.

"If once/we were" was published as a collaboration with M. NourbeSe Philip in spacecraftprojects: https://spacecraftproject.files.wordpress.com/2019/10/collaboration -nourbese-phillip-and-j-otok-bitek.pdf

"There's something about ... Vancouver" was published in *The Capilano Review* 3.38 (2019) as "Something about #1."
"There's something about ... Today" was published in *Gauntlet* (Nomados Press, 2019) as "Gentlemen, start your engine."
"There's something about ... Thick sludge" was commissioned for the 2020 Fraser Valley Literary Festival as "Something about #3."

"Jacob's breath" was first published in *Room* 44.1 (2020).

"The lock poems" were written during a writing residency at Capilano University with additional support & love from the folks at *The Capilano Review*.

"Gari ya moshi" is a children's song from Kibera.

"Exterminate the brutes!" is quoted from Joseph Conrad's *Heart of Darkness*. I trace my literary journey of this line through *Things Fall Apart* (Chinua Achebe), *Apocalypse Now* (Francis Ford Coppola) & *The Thing Around Your Neck* (Chimamanda Ngozi Adichie).

Credits for details of numbers & places around slavery & colonialism in Acholi to Okot p'Bitek's Ph.D. thesis entitled "Oral literature and its social background among the Acholi and Lango," Oxford University, 1963.

A version of "Salt stories" was initially published in Room 40.3 (2018) as "Migration: Salt stories."

Otoniya J. Okot Bitek is a poet and scholar. Her collection of poetry, *100 Days* (University of Alberta, 2016), was nominated for several writing prizes including the 2017 BC Book Prize, the 2017 Pat Lowther Award, the 2017 Alberta Book Awards and the 2017 Canadian Authors Award for Poetry. It won the 2017 IndieFab Book of the Year Award for poetry and the 2017 Glenna Luschei Prize for African Poetry. From the fall of 2020 to the spring of 2021, Otoniya had the privilege of being the Ellen and Warren Tallman Writer-in-Residence and one of the SFU Jack and Doris Shadbolt Fellows. She has recently moved to Kingston, Ontario, to live on the traditional territory of the Haudenosaunee and Anishinaabe people. Otoniya is an Assistant Professor at Queen's University, Kingston.